The New Kingmakers
How Developers Conquered the World

Stephen O'Grady

Beijing · Cambridge · Farnham · Köln · Sebastopol · Tokyo

THE NEW KINGMAKERS

by Stephen O'Grady

Printed in the United States of America.

Published by O'Reilly Media, Inc., 1005 Gravenstein Highway North, Sebastopol, CA 95472.

O'Reilly books may be purchased for educational, business, or sales promotional use. Online editions are also available for most titles (*http://my.safaribooksonline.com*). For more information, contact our corporate/institutional sales department: (800) 998-9938 or *corporate@oreilly.com*.

January 2013:   First Edition

Revision History for the First Edition:

    2013-01-07:   First release
    2013-01-28:   Second release
    2013-03-15:   Third release

See *http://oreilly.com/catalog/errata.csp?isbn=9781449356347* for release details.

ISBN: 978-1-449-35634-7

To my parents, who taught me to always do my job by always doing theirs.

Contents

Foreword

Not very long ago, developers were primarily seen through the geek lens — as smart people that were too idiosyncratic and unsociable to be taken seriously or capable of wielding much influence. Now that's all changed as developers have attained a new status as the real movers and shakers who hold more power and influence than is known. In high-tech circles, this has opened up an ongoing conversation about how the shifting role of developers is affecting today's IT organizations.

This phenomenon — described with terms like *The Consumerization of IT, The Nerd Economy*, and *The Rise of the Developer* — is what Stephen O'Grady discusses in his book, *The New Kingmakers: How Developers Conquered the World*. In it, Stephen explains how this shift began and how it will shape the future of business, as a whole, in the years to come. He takes a data-driven, realistic look at the new realities facing today's IT organizations and the role that development teams are playing in creating them.

At New Relic, we've written a lot about The Nerd Economy and how it's leading us in a new direction. Developers are now wielding unprecedented power. Polyglot environments, database fragmentation, and cloud and open source adoption are only the beginning. As developers, we are shaping product and user experiences in new ways. And organizations that understand and embrace the value of this shift will be the most successful in the years to come.

Today, developers are unquestionably one of the most important assets a business has, regardless of what industry it is in. This book documents developers' movement out of the shadows and into the light as new influencers on society. It also reveals the larger truth that not just company leaders, but also developers themselves must recognize the role they play in business success. Thus, this new era offers us exciting and unprecedented opportunity: to take pride in our newfound status and ownership of the responsibilities it brings.

—*Lew Cirne*
CEO, New Relic

Introduction

The CIO Is the Last to Know

In 2002, a group of securities-industry CIOs and IT managers were interviewed about their challenges and strategies with regulatory compliance. Specifically, they were asked about their compliance strategies regarding the usage of instant messaging (IM) technologies, a communication channel that predates the Internet, but exploded in popularity as the Web grew. Because IM allows users to communicate quickly and efficiently with each other in real time for free, it found no shortage of users, or use cases — even in the heavily regulated securities industry.

When the executives were interviewed, however, every single one denied that their organization had any compliance obligations with respect to IM. They were certain of this because they were equally certain that IM was not being used. How were they so sure? "We haven't issued those technologies, so they're not being used by our employees," was the typical response. The reality, however, was an unpleasant surprise to these execs. IM technologies might not have been issued by these companies, but with the technologies freely available and highly useful, their use by company employees was rampant and accelerating.

This revelation was to become more and more common over the following decade, however, because the nature of technology adoption was changing. Access to technology has been steadily democratized over the past decade, to the point that, as then CEO of technology provider rPath Billy Marshall put it in 2008, "The CIO is the last to know." The following Venn diagram depicts the current reality in simple fashion.

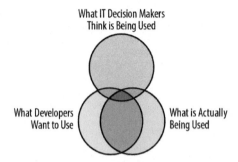

What IT Decision Makers
Think is Being Used

What Developers
Want to Use

What is Actually
Being Used

This recalibration of the practical authority wielded by IT decision makers has profound ramifications for everyone in or around the technology industry, as well as those businesses that consume technology — which today is virtually every business.

For years, medium-to-large-sized businesses — colloquially referred to as "enterprise buyers" — were the primary consumers of technology, the economic engine that drove technical innovation. Unsurprisingly, the output of the technology industry reflected these buyers' needs and desires, at the expense of other considerations. Usability was a secondary concern; features like manageability and security were far more important to CIO buyers. Sales and marketing efforts, meanwhile, were crafted around promises of return on investment or labor reduction, rather than personal appeal. There's a reason the iPhone is an order of magnitude easier to use than the average business software application. Apple needed to convince each customer on the virtues of a given device. Enterprise technology vendors needed to sell only to the one buying the software. If the employees found the products difficult to use, so be it.

In an industry where usage is a function of purchase rather than a real desire for the item, technology providers will obviously optimize for the purchasing process. But in reality, that is no longer true today, and hasn't been true for years. As with IM or the iPhone, technology is increasingly being driven by bottom-up, rather than top-down, adoption. The world has changed, but only a select few in the technology industry have realized it. As William Gibson might put it, the future is already here, it's just unevenly distributed.

What does the market think of this new, non-enterprise focused future-present? Currently, Apple is the most valuable technology company in the world, and depending on the price of oil when you read this, the most valuable company in the world, period. As this book goes to press, in fact, Apple is worth more than Adobe, Cisco, Dell, EMC, HP, Oracle, SAP, Red Hat, Sony, and VMware — combined.

In the wake of Apple's unprecedented success, one obvious question remains: if IT decision makers aren't making the decisions any longer, who is calling the shots?

The answer is developers. Developers are the most-important constituency in technology. They have the power to make or break businesses, whether by their preferences, their passions, or their own products.

Consider the "rogue" or "shadow" IT departments that are busily metastasizing within organizations large and small all over the planet, simply because they can. These informal, non-sanctioned IT departments handpick, build, and maintain their own technology stacks — technology stacks into which centralized IT has no visibility, and over which it has no control. The result is a world in which Coca Cola or Ford or JP Morgan aren't the customers any more: their employees are. Vendors are becoming aware that their future relevance and viability will depend not on their salespeoples' willingness to let the CIO beat them at a round of golf, but their ability to get the rank and file to genuinely value their technologies. As we'll see, those that manage this transition most successfully turn sales from a costly and complex negotiation to a fait accompli.

This shift is fundamentally reshaping the industry, and has been doing so for more than a few years — yet many in the industry still fail to fully appreciate how profoundly things have changed. That creates an opportunity for those that do to gain a competitive edge. This shift is fundamentally reshaping the industry, but the appreciation for how profoundly things have changed is asymmetrical. That's surprising, because it has been a decades-long process. But within that asymmetry lies an opportunity.

Geopolitical strategists like Caerus Associates' David Kilcullen talk about how world leaders today need to evolve from negotiating with governments to negotiating with populations. Thanks to technology, populations are better informed, better connected, and better organized than ever before. The entertainment industry discovered this recently when the Stop Online Piracy Act (SOPA) legislation it engineered was defeated by a populist uprising of sorts. As a lobbyist from Ogilvy Government Relations put it, "a well-resourced content group of people completely got outmaneuvered by the guys in the basement."

The technology industry is no exception. The days when you could simply negotiate with a developer's boss are over. Today, you need to court developer populations in the same manner that Apple sells phones: individual by individual.

This book is first about helping you understand this shift and its origins, and second about offering suggestions about how to navigate the changed landscape.

Developers are now the real decision makers in technology. Learning how to best negotiate with these New Kingmakers, therefore, could mean the difference between success and failure.

The New Kingmakers

Buy the Company to Hire the People

Imagine a labor market so tight that recruiting is done via acquisition. This is the reality that the technology industry faces today.

Historically, motivations for merger and acquisition activity in the technology sector have been comparable to that of other industries. Acquisitions typically centered around products, with employees an afterthought. Between January 2002 and January 2012, for example, Oracle acquired 68 companies. The acquisition logic varied, but none were driven purely by talent acquisition. To the contrary: many of these transactions involved acquiring the technology and shedding a majority of the staff.

But this more-rational talent market was the product of an industry dominated by slower-moving enterprise technology vendors. Oracle and other businesses that cater primarily to enterprise buyers are constrained in ways that consumer technology vendors are not. While new services and devices can never arrive quickly enough for consumers, there are upper bounds to the amount and velocity of innovation that enterprises can absorb.

The end result of the rising power and stature of consumer technology vendors is ever higher premiums placed on technical talent. The inevitable byproduct of this greater demand is elevated scarcity. Amidst the worst economic recession since the Great Depression, the talent market for developers has remained historically tight. With the demand for programmers far outstripping the supply, employers are perpetually in search of an edge in recruiting. Perks such as in-office kegorators to no-cost, world-class food have become common as the race to pamper geeks first teetered on the brink, then spiraled out of control. Startup 42Floors, for example, published to their public blog an entry entitled "Consider this a job offer to work at 42Floors." The entry was not a general recruiting pitch, but an actual job offer aimed at a specific developer. An entirely unsolicited job offer for a developer who may or may not have been interested in the job. The opening paragraph:

> *Please join us. Consider this a job offer to work at 42Floors. Because you have never applied for this position, this may come as a little bit of a surprise. But you have known for awhile that I have been really impressed with your work.*

What led 42Floors to this decision? In their own words, "The very best can't be hired. They must be courted." For perhaps the first time in the history of the industry, people are worth more than the code they produce, a valuation supported by logic. Steve Jobs believed that an elite talent was 25 times more valuable to Apple than an average alternative. For Jobs, this was critical to Apple's resurgence:

> *That's probably...certainly the secret to my success. It's that we've gone to exceptional lengths to hire the best people.*

Facebook CEO Mark Zuckerberg agrees, saying in a 2010 interview:

> *Someone who is exceptional in their role is not just a little better than someone who is pretty good. They are 100 times better.*

For Bill Gates, the number was 10,000 times better. If any of these assertions are even approximately correct, the cost of an elite chef or a few kegs of beer pales next to the expected return from the technical talent that these perks could potentially attract. As wildly irrational as these perks might appear to other industries, they are the inevitable product of a high-stakes market long on demand but short on supply.

In 2009, Google's then CEO Eric Schmidt gave an interview to Reuters Television prior to speaking at the G20 Summit. In it, he articulated clearly Google's intent to employ acquisition as a recruitment tactic. "Acquisitions are turned on again at Google and we are doing our normal maneuvers, which is small companies. My estimate would be one-a-month acquisitions and these are largely in lieu of hiring." Translated, this means that even Google, with all its success, its world-class food, its 20% time, and its high-end recruiters, cannot hire enough talent to meet its growth targets. Schmidt was as good as his word, as Google's recent acquisitions include startups Aardvark, AppJet, Apture, Like.com, reMail, and Slide. None of the products of those startups remain available.

Nor is Google alone. Virtually all of the Silicon Valley consumer technology firms have begun to engage in this practice. Industry sentiment, for example, suggests that Facebook acquired Beluga, Daytum, Digital Staircase, Drop.io, Friend-

Feed, Gowalla, Hot Potato, MailRank, Parakey, Snaptu, and Strobe for their employees rather than their technology. Twitter, for its part, has snapped up Backtype, Dasient, Fluther, Hotspot.io, Julpan, Summize, and Whisper Systems; LinkedIn, ChoiceVendor, IndexTank, and Mspoke; Zynga, Area/Code, and Unoh; GroupOn, Pelago, and Uptake; Amazon, TeachStreet.

This practice is so widespread that a term, *acqhiring*, has entered the industry lexicon to describe it. Even for the skeptics, it's difficult to argue that these acquisitions are about anything other than people. In many deals, like Facebook's acquisition of Gowalla, the technology was not even a part of the transaction. And when the technology is included in the transaction, it is frequently released as open source post-acquisition.

The people, by contrast, are the real asset. Facebook's 2008 acquisition of FriendFeed, for example, cost the company $50 million dollars. How did Facebook justify the acquisition? "We really wanted to get Bret [Taylor]," said Mark Zuckerberg of the man who is now Facebook's CTO. Joe Hewitt, meanwhile, who came in the Parakey acquisition, wrote Facebook's first iPhone application. And Gowalla's Josh Williams is now the product manager for locations and events at Facebook.

In spite of the premiums and the obvious inefficiency of practices like acqhiring, there is no evidence that the labor market will equalize in the near term. Given this perpetual shortage, we can expect employers to go to ever greater lengths to adapt: up to and including acquiring.

What Are Developers Worth? A DOJ Suit

According to the Department of Justice, from 2005 to 2010, Intel would not hire you if you worked for Google. Google, in turn, would not hire you if you worked for Apple. Nor would Pixar, who also would not hire you if you worked for Lucas-Film. Predictably, these alleged practices caught the attention of federal regulators, who opened an investigation. In 2010, the DOJ filed a civil antitrust complaint against six technology companies, alleging that they colluded to artificially depress the jobs market by limiting employee mobility. By the DOJ's account, this situation was the product of agreements — both written and of the handshake variety — between the heads of large technology vendors who promised not to poach employees from one another. These agreements might not have been legally enforceable, but they nevertheless stalled the technology employment market for years. Six large technology vendors eventually settled with the DOJ, and developers were once more free to move at will.

The rationale behind these extra-legal machinations was simple: developers had become too valuable. In a market where employees were able to move without restriction from one Silicon Valley company to another, standard recruitment practices would logically result in both higher turnover and an unsustainable salary escalation. Instead, according to the DOJ, vendors colluded to artificially depress the developer marketplace by limiting employee mobility. Besides being illegal, this practice is perhaps the best indication yet of the value attached to technologists, as companies are in effect saying: "developers are so valuable we will act illegally to retain them."

The non-hiring pact seems to suggest that companies like Apple, Google, and Intel agree with the high valuation Bill Gates, Steve Jobs, and Mark Zuckerberg place on the most skilled developers, but what about the world outside of Silicon Valley? There, too, the valuation of developers is at an all-time high. In New York City, for example, traditional financial services employers are competing with industries like advertising, healthcare, and even defense over developers with strong quantitative analysis skills. Why? Because virtually every business today is a technology business on some level.

Everywhere you turn, developers are in high demand. What about what they produce?

The People vs The Code

If developers are valuable enough to break labor laws for, what of the software that they create? What software is worth is, in fact, among the fundamental questions facing the market today. Industry opinions on the subject vary, but public markets hold no great opinion of the technology industry broadly. Apple may be the most valuable company in the world now, but it wasn't in *Fortune's* Top Ten last year. Nor was any other technology vendor. Even within the context of the software industry, there are indications that the market is pessimistic about the potential returns realizable through software. A software analog to the Fortune 500, the PricewaterhouseCoopers (PwC) Global 100, ranks software vendors worldwide by revenue. The salient detail is the age of the companies. Remarkably, none of the vendors in the Top 20 of the PwC ranking were founded after 1989. The mean age of the companies on the list, in fact, is 47 years. In other words, the market is not creating new big businesses that sell software — the biggest software businesses were all created decades ago.

On some level, this is no surprise. Using acquisition as a means to outsource risk is a business practice with a long history that reaches far beyond the technology sector. Big companies pay a premium for small companies in order to acquire new resources, processes, business models, or all of the above. This explanation fails to account for current market conditions, however. For one, it cannot account for the fact that two of the top three technology vendors by market cap — Apple and Microsoft — are on the younger side of the mean. But more problematically, it obscures the importance of Google. The search vendor is not included in PwC's Top 20 software vendors by revenue, presumably because it is not primarily in the business of selling software. If we were to compare their market cap, however, to the top five vendors on the PwC list, they would place fourth, just behind Oracle. In other words, some of the biggest software firms aren't considered software firms because they're making money with software, not from it. Their software isn't the commercial asset, but merely an enabler to an alternative business model.

It would seem that we've come full circle in the valuations attached to code. Three decades ago at what might be considered the dawn of the modern era of computing, IBM put little value in the development of an operating system, and Microsoft capitalized. The importance of software soon became apparent, and the Redmond-based vendor rode it to a near-$400 billion market capitalization in the late nineties. For the tech-sector powerhouses that have reached prominence since then, however, the money hasn't been in software, but what they could build with software. That was true for Google, and now appears to be true for Facebook, the youngest of the Internet giants. A high percentage of Facebook's internal technical innovation is released as open source software, a strong indication that the company places little value in protecting its software.

Where businesses once saw outsized returns from the code they wrote, today it's merely a means to an end. It's often not even a competitive advantage. What does this mean for those in the commercial software business? When considered in the context of acqhiring, it means that people are increasingly more valuable than the software they produce.

3

How Did We Get Here

The Disruptors

In the latter half of the 20th century, developers were effectively beholden to their employers. The tools they needed to be productive — hardware and software — just were not affordable on an individual basis. Developers wishing to build even something as trivial as a website were confronted by an unfortunate reality: most of the necessary building blocks were available only under commercial licenses. Operating systems, databases, web and application servers, and development tools all required money. To get anything done, developers needed someone to write checks for the tools they needed. That meant either raising the capital to buy the necessary pieces, or — more often — requesting that an employer or other third party purchase them on the developer's behalf.

The new century, however, has ushered in profound and permanent shifts in the relationship between developer and employer. No longer is the former at the mercy of the latter's budget. With the cost of development down by an order of magnitude or more, the throttle on developer creativity has been removed, setting the stage for a Cambrian explosion of projects.

Four major disruptions drove this shift: open source, the cloud, the Internet, and seed-stage financing.

The Symbiosis of Open Source and Developers

The phrase "open source" did not yet exist in 1995, when the first versions of the Apache web server and MySQL database were being written. It was coined in 1998, when the world needed a way to describe the public release of the Netscape browser's source code.

Nearly two decades later, open source projects are ubiquitous. The two most-popular web servers in the world — Apache and Nginx — are open source, as is the most-popular relational database (MySQL). The most-popular mobile platform in the world, Android, is another open source project. A company that sells only open source software, Red Hat, crossed the billion-dollar revenue threshold for the first time in 2011. Open source built one $100-billion-plus business — Google — and it's providing the infrastructure for the next would-be contender — Facebook — which regularly releases pieces of its core infrastructure. Even Forrester and Gartner, industry observers that focus on conservative IT buyers, have concluded that open source has achieved mainstream traction, saying "Mainstream adopters of IT solutions across a widening array of market segments are rapidly gaining confidence in the use of open source software."

The success of these projects and others like them is thanks to developers. The millions of programmers across the world who use, develop, improve, document, and rely upon open source are the main reason it's relevant, and the main reason it continues to grow. In return for this support, open source has set those developers free from traditional procurement. Forever.

Financial constraints that once served as a barrier to entry in software not only throttled the rate and pace of innovation in the industry, they ensured that organizational developers were a subservient class at best, a cost center at worst. With the rise of open source, however, developers could for the first time assemble an infrastructure from the same pieces that industry titans like Google used to build their businesses — only at no cost, without seeking permission from anyone. For the first time, developers could route around traditional procurement with ease. With usage thus effectively decoupled from commercial licensing, patterns of technology adoption began to shift.

From the collapse of the commercial development tools business to the rise of Linux, open source software has disrupted and destroyed one commercial software market after another. At the same time, open source has created brand-new businesses such as Facebook, Google, and Twitter, none of which could have born the up-front capital expense cost structures associated with traditional commercial software licensing. Cowen & Co analyst Peter Goldmacher estimated that the capital expenses associated with building YouTube on top of Oracle's Exadata platform would cost $589 million, or $485 million more than it would to build it from software it could obtain for free.

Armed with software they could obtain with or without approval, developers were on their way to being the most-important constituency in technology. All that they lacked was similarly frictionless access to hardware.

Hardware for Pennies an Hour?

Even with a growing portfolio of high-quality open source software available to them, developers remained limited by the availability of hardware. As creative as they could now be with their software infrastructure, to build anything of size, they would eventually have to procure hardware. This meant either purchasing it outright or renting it, typically for the minimum of a month, with the attendant set up, management, and maintenance fees on top.

Enter Amazon Web Services (AWS). The idea was simple. Driven relentlessly by Moore's Law, hardware doubled in speed every two years. Like Google and other Internet giants, Amazon discovered early that the most-economical model for scaling its technology was on cheap, commodity servers deployed by the hundreds or thousands. Having acquired the expertise to build, run, and manage these machines at scale, Amazon would leverage the same as a product. The volatile demands of the infrastructure needed to run its retail business ensured both favorable economies of scale as well as hard-won lessons learned in coping with extreme scale.

Leveraging open source virtualization technologies and other no-cost pieces of infrastructure, Amazon introduced EC2 (the Elastic Compute Cloud) and S3 (the Simple Storage Service) in 2006. Though primitive at first, these services were nevertheless revolutionary, offering developers the opportunity to purchase hardware on demand, paying only for what they used. Anyone with a credit card could rent hardware and storage space, dynamically, for minutes, hours, months, or years.

Practically speaking, AWS, and the cloud market it created, removed the final cost constraint on developer creativity. As Flip Kromer, CTO of data startup Infochimps put it, "EC2 means anyone with a $10 bill can rent a 10-machine cluster with 1TB of distributed storage for 8 hours." For all of the focus on the technology of cloud computing, its real import has been the elimination of up-front capital expense costs and making any class of hardware instantly accessible. Hardware had certainly been available via a network before, but never this cheaply, and never in such an on-demand fashion.

With the creation of the cloud market, developers had, for the first time in history, access to both no-cost software and infrastructure affordable for even an individual. As the capital expenses associated with business creation fell precipitously, the volume of new businesses exploded. PHPFog's Head of Marketing Chris Tacy's research on venture funding over the last decade clearly displays the impact. After 2006, the drop in average deal sizes is offset by a spike in deal volume.

Total Angel/Venture Deals vs Average Deal Size

|2001 2002 2003 2004 2005 2006 2007 2008 2009 2010|

— Normalized Total Deals   — Normalized Deal Size

The implication is obvious: as the capital expenses associated with business creation fell, the deal volume spiked. In other words, because it was cheaper to start a business, more businesses got started.

Cloud uptake was not unique to startups, of course. Thousands of traditional businesses have been consuming cloud services, whether they realize it or not, because of the lower cost, greater availability, the elasticity, or all of the above. Once cloud services became widely available at affordable prices, the last obstacle between a developer and his tools was gone. Hardware was now just as available as software, and almost as cheap. With the tools in hand, all that developers needed was guidance on how to use them and economic opportunities to do so.

Harnessing the Power of the Internet

Before the Internet existed, developers had roles — roles of importance. But their independence and ability to maximize their value was limited by inefficiencies in the non-digital networks they used to educate themselves, market themselves, and sell their skills or products. As it has in many other industries, the Internet has made these processes radically more efficient, rewarding developers in the process.

In the 1980s and 1990s, freelance developers were far rarer than they are today. Freelancing was particularly difficult for developers who lacked an uncommon, niche skillset. It was hard for developers to market themselves — not that self-promotion was very high on the typical developer's priority list to begin with. That in turn made finding projects problematic. Blogging was one early vehicle that developers employed to overcome this problem. Developers who regularly published details of their work and their projects were able to build a following of both like-minded developers as well as potential employers. As independent Java developer Matt Raible put it in 2006:

> The biggest fear that folks have about "going independent" is they'll have a hard time finding their next gig. If you're productive and blog about what you're doing, this shouldn't be a problem. I haven't had an "interview" since 2002 and haven't updated my resume since then either.

Since then, a variety of tools have appeared that complement the blog as developer marketing vehicles. Developers using Twitter, for example, can easily build large networks that can effectively route availability and skills information to large audiences of potential employers. While not primarily a developer tool, LinkedIn can serve similar purposes for some specific skillsets. And GitHub may be the truest marketing opportunity of all, because publishing source code openly allows developers to demonstrate their hard skills. Word of mouth has never been more efficient than it is today.

Markets for developers and their services have also been made more efficient by the Internet. Thousands of businesses now hire contractors through basic properties like Craigslist or developer-specific sites like Elance or oDesk. Even Google's Apps Marketplace includes a Professional Services section. The benefits to developer and employer alike are obvious: discovery, project management, and payment have become much more efficient.

And for developers who choose to market and sell products, there are numerous online venues ready to retail their wares for commissions ranging from 20% to 40%. If you're selling mobile applications, Apple's App Store has already distributed 25 billion applications. Android developers, meanwhile, can count on an addressable market that's activating 1.3 million new devices per day. Amazon, Microsoft, and RIM all have their own equivalents as well. Over on the desktop, Apple, Canonical, and Microsoft are or will soon be offering the ability to sell applications to users. The same is true for Software-as-a-Service; platforms like Google or Jive are increasingly offering their own "app stores," giving developers or third parties the opportunity to sell to their customers.

Marketing and selling yourself or the applications you've built requires training, obviously. Historically, this has been a challenge. While motivated individuals could learn through texts and manuals or, if they could afford it, computer-based training, none duplicated the experience of being taught by your peers, on the job, in part because few of the available learning mechanisms were interactive. Today, that is no longer the case. Sites like Stack Overflow or Quora allow developers to interact directly and collaboratively with each other, asking and answering each other's questions quickly and easily. GitHub allows them to contribute directly to each other's code — one reason the site's motto is "Social Coding." And open source has long been a proving ground for new developers.

Although offering less interaction, the flow of pure educational resources to the Internet is accelerating. Stanford has been aggressively pushing their class content to the Web: from curricula to actual lectures, would-be developers all over the world are able to receive some of the benefits of a world-class education, at no cost. And beginning in the Fall of 2012, edX will educate students with Harvard and MIT course content — for free. The program, a $60-million-dollar collaboration between the two universities, aims to expand their addressable market to students anywhere. Startups are targeting similar opportunities: for example, CodeAcademy aims to teach anyone coding, while Khan Academy's broader mandate includes a spectrum of computer science and math classes. Even commercial vendors like Cisco, IBM, Microsoft, and SAP have devoted substantial budgets to properties aimed at educating developers.

The relentless efficiency of the Internet, the bane of industries like publishing, has been a boon to developers. They're more visible and marketable than ever, demand for their services is skyrocketing, and their commercial opportunities are more frictionless than ever before.

The New Money Lenders

Though open source reduced or eliminated the cost of software and the pay-as-you-go cloud model made it possible to obtain hardware for a fraction of its historical up-front cost, there's no escaping the fact that startups cost money. From hardware to healthcare, snacks to salaries, even modest startups have bills to pay.

Some entrepreneurial developers bootstrap themselves via a product or by moonlighting as consultants and contractors. But others seek capital so they can focus on their young companies without distraction. Historically, the funding options available to these entrepreneurs have been limited — angel investors are few and far between, which left only loans from friends, family, banks, or credit unions. Even when venture capitalists took an interest, the deals they offered often were not favorable for entrepreneurs — they frequently provided more money than was required in order to obtain the largest possible share of the company.

Then in 2008, Paul Graham's Y Combinator launched. Recognizing that the technology landscape had dramatically lowered the cost of starting a business, Y Combinator offered substantially less money — typically less than $20,000 — in return for a commensurately smaller share of the company. Its average equity stake was around 6%. The falling costs of business creation led to a decoupling of the average deal size with the average deal volume. Because the changing technology landscape had dramatically lowered the cost of starting a technology business, its small investments were sufficient to get these young companies off the ground. With the amount of money each company needed in decline, more businesses were given less money, and Y Combinator and other programs like TechStars have played a critical role in this.

Seed-stage investment funds democratized access to capital much as the cloud lowered the friction associated with hardware acquisition and open source erased the barriers between developers and software. The result? Businesses like Dropbox, which turned down a nine-digit offer from Steve Jobs and subsequently raised money at a four-billion-dollar valuation.

For developers that don't wish to surrender any control, Kickstarter represents yet another funding option. Founded in 2008, Kickstarter is a crowd source funding platform that had attracted $175 million in contributions as of April 2012. The model is simple: for a commission of 5% on each project — and a few additional percentage points due Amazon for usage of their payments network — Kickstarter provides artists, filmmakers, developers, and others with a direct line to potential individual investors. Unlike traditional venture capital, however, Kickstarter claims no ownership stake in funded projects — all rights are retained by the project owners.

Though Kickstarter is by no means focused strictly on developers, they have been among the most impressive beneficiaries. Of the top projects by funds raised, the first three are video games. In March 2012, Double Fine Adventure set the record for Kickstarter projects, attracting $3.3 million in crowd-sourced financing. Number two on the list, Wasteland 2, raised just under $3 million, with third place Shadowrun Returns receiving $1.8 million. The Kickstarter model is less established than even seed-stage venture dollars, but it shows every sign of being a powerful funding option for developers moving forward.

In little more than a decade, developers had gained access to free software, affordable hardware, powerful networking tools, and more entrepreneur-friendly financing options. Things would never be the same again.

4

The Evidence

What Would a Developer's World Look Like?

If members of the newly empowered developer class really are the New Kingmakers, shaping their own destiny and increasingly setting the technical agenda, how could we tell? What would happen if developers could choose their technologies, rather than having them chosen for them?

- First, there would be greater technical diversity. Where enterprises tend to consolidate their investments in as few technologies as possible (according to the "one throat to choke" model) developers, as individuals, are guided by their own preferences rather than a corporate mandate. Because they're more inclined to use the best tool for the job, a developer-dominated marketplace would demonstrate a high degree of fragmentation.

- Second, open source would grow and proliferate. Whether it's because they enjoy the collaboration, abhor unnecessary duplication of effort, because they're building a resume of code, because they find it easy to obtain, or because it costs them nothing, developers prefer open source over proprietary commercial alternatives in the majority of cases. If developers were calling the shots, we'd expect to see open source demonstrating high growth.

- Third, developers would ignore or bypass vendor-led, commercially oriented technical standards efforts. Corporate-led standards tend to be designed by committee, with consensus and buy-in from multiple parties required prior to sign off. Like any product of a committee, standards designed in this fashion tend to be over-complicated and over-architected. This complexity places an overhead on developers who must then learn the standard before they can leverage it. Given that developers would, like any of us, prefer the simplest path, a world controlled by developers would see simple, organic standards triumphing over vendor-backed, artificially constructed alternatives.

- Last, technology vendors would prostrate themselves in an effort to court developers. If developers are materially important to their respective businesses, they'd be behaving accordingly, making it easier for them to build relationships with technologists.

As it happens, all four of these things that would happen in this theoretical developer-led world have happened in the real world.

Choice and Fragmentation

Not too long ago, conventional wisdom dictated that enterprises strictly limit themselves to one of two competing technology stacks — Java or .NET. But in truth, the world was never that simple. While the Sun vs Microsoft storyline supplied journalists with the sort of one-on-one rivalry they love to mine, the reality was never so black and white. Even as the enterprises focused on the likes of J2EE, Perl, PHP, and others were flowing like water around the "approved" platforms, servicing workloads where development speed and low barriers to entry were at a premium. It was similar to what had occurred years earlier, when Java and C# supplanted the platforms (C, C++, etc.) that preceded them.

Fragmentation in the language and platform space is nothing new: "different tools for different jobs" has always been the developers' mantra, if not that of the buyers supplying them. But the pace of this fragmentation is accelerating, with the impacts downstream significantly less clear.

Today, Java and .NET remain widely used. But they're now competing with a dozen competitive languages, not just one or two. Newly liberated developers are exercising their newfound freedoms, aggressively employing languages once considered "toys" compared to the more traditional and enterprise-approved environments. By my firm RedMonk's metrics, Java and C# — the .NET stack's primary development language — are but two of the languages our research considers Tier 1 (see below). JavaScript, PHP, Python, and Ruby in particular have exploded in popularity over the last few years and are increasingly finding a place even within conservative enterprises. Elsewhere, languages like CoffeeScript and Scala, which were designed to be more accessible versions of JavaScript and Java, respectively, are demonstrating substantial growth.

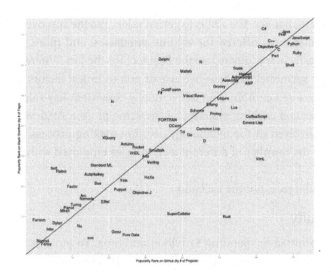

Nor are programming language stacks the only technology category experiencing fragmentation. Even the database market is decentralizing. Since their invention in the late 1960s and the subsequent popularization in the 1970s, relational databases have been the dominant form of persisting information. From an application-development perspective, relational databases were the answer regardless of the question. Oracle, IBM, and Microsoft left little oxygen for other would-be participants in the database space, and they collectively ensured that virtually every application deployed was backed by a relational database. This dominance, fueled in part by enterprise conservatism, was sustained for decades.

The first crack in the armor came with the arrival of open source alternatives. MySQL in particular leveraged free availability and an easier-to-use product to become the most-popular database in the world. But for all of its popularity, it was quite similar to the commercial products it competed with: it was, in the end, another relational database. And while the relational model is perfect for many tasks, it is obviously not perfect for every task.

When web-native firms like Facebook and Google helped popularize infrastructures composed of hundreds of small servers rather than a few very big ones, developers began to perceive some of the limitations of this relational database model. Some of them went off and created their own new databases that were distinctly non-relational in their design. The result today is a vibrant, diverse market of non-relational databases optimized for almost any business need.

CIOs choose software according to a number of different factors. Quality of technology is among them, but they are also concerned with the number of vendor relationships a business has to manage, the ability to get a vendor onto the approved-supplier lists, the various discounts offered for volume purchases, and more. A developer, by contrast, typically just wants to use the best tool for the job. Where a CIO might employ a single relational database because of non-technical factors, a developer might instead turn to a combination of eventually consistent key value stores, in memory databases and caching systems for the same project. As developers have become more involved in the technology decision-making process, it has been no surprise to see the number of different technologies employed within a given business skyrocket.

Fragmentation is now the rule, not the exception.

Open Source and Ubiquity

In 2001, IBM publicly committed to spending $1 billion on Linux. To put this in context, that figure represented 1.2% of the company's revenue that year and a fifth of its entire 2001 R&D spend. Between porting its own applications to Linux and porting Linux to its hardware platforms, IBM, one of the largest commercial technology vendors on the planet, was pouring a billion dollars into the ecosystem around an operating system originally written by a Finnish graduate student that no single entity — not even IBM — could ever own. By the time IBM invested in the technology, Linux was already the product of years of contributions from individual developers and businesses all over the world.

How did this investment pan out? A year later, Bill Zeitler, head of IBM's server group, claimed that they'd made almost all of that money back. "We've recouped most of it in the first year in sales of software and systems. We think it was money well spent. Almost all of it, we got back."

Linux has defied the predictions of competitors like Microsoft and traditional analyst firms alike to become a worldwide phenomenon, and a groundbreaking success. Today it powers everything from Android devices to IBM mainframes. All of that would mean little if it were the exception that proved the rule. Instead Linux has paved the way for enterprise acceptance of open source software. It's difficult to build the case that open source isn't ready for the enterprise when Linux is the default operating system of your datacenters.

Linux was the foundation of LAMP, a collection of operating system, web server, programming language, and database software that served as an alternative to solutions from Microsoft, among others. Lightweight, open source, and well suited to a variety of tasks, LAMP was propelled to worldwide fame by the developers who loved it. The effects of their affection can still be seen. The March 2012 Netcraft survey found that Apache was on 65.24% of the more than 644 million servers surveyed worldwide. The next closest competitor was Microsoft's Internet Information Server — at 13.81%. MySQL, meanwhile, was sufficiently ubiquitous that in order to acquire it with the EU's regulatory approval, Oracle was compelled to make a series of promises, among them a commitment to continue developing the product. And while PHP is competing in an increasingly crowded landscape, it powers tens of millions of websites around the world, and is the fifth most-popular programming language as of March 2012 as measured by Ohloh, a code-monitoring site.

Beyond LAMP, open source is increasingly the default mode of software development. For example, Java, once closed source software, was strategically open sourced in an effort to both widen its appeal and remain competitive. Companies developing software, meanwhile, are open sourcing their internal development efforts at an accelerating rate. In new market categories, open source is the rule, proprietary software the exception. In the emerging non-relational database market, for example, the most popular and adopted projects are all open source. Mike Stonebreaker, the founder of seven different database companies, told the GlueCon conference audience in 2010 that it was impossible to be a new project in the database space without being open source.

The ascendance of open source is not altruistic; it's simply good business for contributors and consumers alike. But the reason it's good business is that it makes developers happier, more productive, and more efficient.

Standards: Who Decides?

When Mosaic Communications Corporation was renamed Netscape in November 1994, the Web was still mostly an idea. Google was four years from incorporating, ten away from its public offering, and twelve from becoming a verb in the Oxford English Dictionary. Not only was Facebook not yet invented, Mark Zuckerberg wasn't even in high school yet. It's difficult to even recall in these latter days what life was like before the largest information network the world has ever seen became available all the time, on devices that hadn't been invented yet.

The large technology vendors may not have understood the potential — there were few who did — but they at least knew enough to hedge their bets with the World Wide Web. IBM obtained the IBM.com domain in March 1986. Oracle would follow with its own .com in December 1988, as would Microsoft in May of 1991. For businesses that had evolved to sell technology to businesses, it was difficult to grasp the wider implications of a public Internet. At Microsoft, in fact, it took an internal email from Bill Gates — subject line "The Internet Tidal Wave" — to wake up the software giant to the opportunity.

By the time Google followed in Altavista's footsteps, however, the desire for large vendors to extend their businesses to the Web was strong. Strong enough that they were willing to put their traditional animosity aside and collaborate on standards around what was being referred to as "web services."

Eventually encompassing more than a hundred separate standards, web services pushed by the likes of IBM, Microsoft, and Sun Microsystems were an attempt by the technology industry to transform the public Internet into something that looked more like a corporate network. From SOAP to WS-Discovery to WS-Inspection to WS-Interoperability to WS-Notification to WS-Policy to WS Reliable Messaging to WS-ReliableMessaging (not a typo, Reliable Messaging and ReliableMessaging are different standards) to WS-Transfer, for every potential business use case, there was a standard, maintained by a standards body like OASIS or the W3C, and developed by large enterprise technology vendors.

It made perfect sense to the businesses involved: the Internet was a peerless network, but one they found lacking, functionally. And rather than have each vendor solve this separately, and worse — incompatibly — the vendors would collaborate on solutions that would be publicly available, and vendor agnostic by design.

There was just one problem: developers ignored the standards.

This development should have surprised no one. While the emerging standards made sense for specialized business use cases, they were generally irrelevant to individual developers. Worse, there were more than a hundred standards, each with its own set of documentation — and the documentation for each standard often exceeded a hundred pages. What made sense from the perspective of a business made no sense whatsoever to the legions of developers actually building the Web. Among developers, the web services efforts were often treated as a punchline. David Heinemeier Hansson, the creator of the popular Ruby on Rails web framework, referred to them as the "WS-Deathstar."

Beyond the inherent difficulties of pushing dozens of highly specialized, business-oriented specifications onto an unwilling developer population, the WS-* set of standards had to contend with an alternative called Representational State Transfer (REST). Originally introduced and defined by Roy Fielding in 2000 in his doctoral dissertation, REST was everything that WS-* was not. Fielding, one the authors of HTTP, the protocol that still powers the Internet today — you've probably typed http:// many times yourself — advocated for a simple style that both reflected and leveraged the way the Internet itself had been constructed. Unsurprisingly, this simpler approach proved popular.

At Amazon, for example, developers were able to choose between the two different mechanisms to access data: SOAP or REST. Even in 2004, 80% of those leveraging Amazon Web Services did so via REST. Two years after that, Google deprecated their SOAP API for search. And they were just the beginning.

It's hard to feel too sorry for SOAP's creators, however — particularly if what one Microsoft developer told Tim O'Reilly is true: "It was actually a Microsoft objective to make [SOAP] sufficiently complex that only the tools would read and write this stuff," he explained, "and not humans."

But it's important to understand the impact. By the latter half of the last decade, the writing was on the wall. Even conservative, CIO-oriented analyst firms were acknowledging REST's role and the weaknesses of the vendor-led WS-* set of standards. The Gartner Group's Nick Gall went so far as to attack the WS-* stack, saying the following in 2007:

> Web Services based on SOAP and WSDL are "Web" in name only. In fact, they are a hostile overlay of the Web based on traditional enterprise middleware architectural styles that has fallen far short of expectations over the past decade.

Companies like eBay that were founded when SOAP looked as if it would persist (in spite of developer distaste for it) have largely continued to support these APIs alongside REST alternatives in order to avoid breaking the application built on them. But few businesses that were founded after SOAP's popularity peaked offer anything but REST or REST-style interfaces. From ESPN to Facebook to Twitter, these businesses' APIs reject the complexity of the WS-* stack, favoring the more-basic mechanism of HTTP transport. The Programmable Web, a website that serves as a directory for APIs, reports that as of March 2012, 71% of the 5,287 APIs were REST based. Less than a fifth were SOAP.

Protocol Usage by APIs

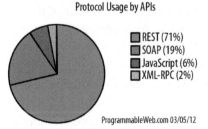

- REST (71%)
- SOAP (19%)
- JavaScript (6%)
- XML-RPC (2%)

ProgrammableWeb.com 03/05/12

The market spoke, and even the vendors pushing competitive protocols had to listen. The market-wide acceptance of REST was a major victory for developers. Besides the practical implications — a Web that remained free of over-architected web services interfaces — the success of REST was a symbol. For perhaps the first time in the history of the technology industry, the actual practitioners were able to subvert and ultimately sideline the product of a massive, cross-industry enterprise technology consortium.

Which is why today, REST or the even simpler approaches it gave rise to dominate the Web.

Courting the Developer Population

GETTING IT RIGHT

Historically, appreciation for the importance of developers has been uneven, as have been corporate efforts to court the developer population. Developers require a distinct, specific set of incentives and resources. Here are five businesses that, in at least one area, understood the importance of developers and engaged appropriately.

APPLE

In August 2011, a month after reporting record earnings, Apple surpassed Exxon as the world's biggest company by market capitalization. This benchmark was reached in part because of fluctuations in oil price that affected Exxon's valuation, but there's little debate that Apple is ascendant. By virtually any metric, Steve Jobs's second tenure at Apple has turned into one of the most successful in history, in any industry.

Seamlessly moving from hit product to hit product, the Apple of 2012 looks nothing like the Apple of the late nineties, when Dell CEO Michael Dell famously suggested that Apple should be shut down, to "give the money back to the shareholders." It is no longer the leader in smartphone shipments, but according to independent analyst Horace Dediu, Apple regularly collects two-thirds of the industry's total available mobile phone profits. Meanwhile, its dominance of the tablet market is so overwhelming that it's being called "unbeatable" by industry observers. Which isn't surprising, since a standalone iPad revenue stream would place it in the top third of Fortune 500 businesses. Even its forgotten desktop business is showing steady if unspectacular growth.

There are many factors contributing to Apple's remarkable success, from the brilliance of the late Steve Jobs to the supply chain sophistication of current CEO

Tim Cook. And of course, Apple's success is itself fueling more success. In the tablet market, for example, would-be competitors face not only the daunting task of countering Apple's unparalleled hardware and software design abilities, but the economies of scale that allow Apple to buy components more cheaply than anyone else. The perfect storm of Apple's success is such that some analysts are forecasting that it could become the world's first trillion-dollar company.

Lost in the shuffle has been the role of developers in Apple's success. But while the crucial role played by Apple's developers in the company's success might be lost on the mainstream media, it is not lost on Apple itself. In March 2012, Apple dedicated the real estate on its website to the following graphic.

Setting aside the 25 billion applications milestone for a moment, consider the value of the home page. For a major retailer to devote the front page of a website to anything other than product is unusual. This action implies that Apple expects to reap tangible benefits from thanking its developers — most notably when it comes to recruiting additional developers. Clothed in this humble "thank you" is a sub-liminal message aimed at those building for its platform: develop for Apple, and you can sell in great volume.

As a rule, developers want the widest possible market. If they're selling soft-ware, a larger audience means more potential sales. But even if they're developing for reasons other than profit, a larger market can mean better visibility for their code — and that, in turn, can translate into higher consulting rates, job offers, and more. By emphasizing their enormous volume, Apple is actively reminding devel-opers that tens of thousands of other developers have already decided to build for iOS and been successful in doing it. If you're going to market to developers, this is how you do it. Subtly, and based on success.

Apple obviously realizes just how important developers are to its success. It's hard to remember now, but there was a time when there wasn't "an app for that." When the iPhone was first released, it didn't run third-party applications: the only applications available were those that came standard on the phone. It wasn't until a year later that Apple released a software development kit (SDK) for developers to begin building applications for the hardware. By 2009, a mere two years after the iPhone was launched, Apple was running the ads that would turn "there's an app for that" into the cliché it is today.

While Apple's application strategy has unquestionably been crucial to the success to date of the iPad and iPhone — not to mention the developers who've earned $4 billion via the App Store — it's the higher switching costs created by Apple's application strategy that might be of greater long-term importance. In their book *Information Rules*, Haas School of Business Professor Carl Shapiro and Google Chief Economist Hal Varian claim that "the profits you can earn from a customer — on a going forward, present-value basis — exactly equal the total switching costs." This, more than Apple's design abilities, and even more than its supply chain excellence, may be the real concern for would-be Apple competitors. Each application downloaded onto an iPad — particularly each app purchased — is one more powerful reason not to defect to a competitive platform like Android or Windows Mobile. An iPhone or iPad user contemplating a switch would have to evaluate whether they can get all of the same applications on a competitive platform, then decide whether they're willing to purchase the commercial apps a second time for a different platform.

Apple has, with its success, created a virtuous cycle that will continue to reward it for years to come. Developers are attracted to its platform because of the size of the market...those developers create thousands of new applications...the new applications give consumers thousands of additional reasons to buy Apple devices rather than the competition...and those new Apple customers give even more developers reason to favor Apple. Apple not only profits from this virtuous cycle, it benefits from ever-increasing economies of scale, realizing lower component costs than competitors.

None of which would be possible without the developers Apple has recruited and, generally, retained.

AMAZON WEB SERVICES

The company that started the cloud computing craze was founded in 1994 as a bookstore. The quintessential Internet company, Amazon.com competed with the traditional brick-and-mortar model via an ever-expanding array of technical innovations: some brilliant, others mundane. The most-important of Amazon's retail innovations co-opted its customers into contributors. From affiliate marketing programs to online reviews, Amazon used technology to enable its customers' latent desire to more fully participate in the buying process. The world's largest retailer was, by design, a bottom-up story from the beginning. It was also, by necessity, a technology company. The combination is why Amazon is the most-underrated threat to the enterprise technology sector on the planet.

In 2006, Amazon's Web Services (AWS) division introduced two new services called the Elastic Compute Cloud (EC2) and Simple Storage Service (S3). These services, elemental in their initial form, were difficult to use, limited in functionality, but breathtakingly cheap — my first bill from Amazon Web Services was for $0.12. From such humble beginnings came what we today call *the cloud*. Today, there are sizable businesses — a great many of them, in fact — that run their infrastructure off of machines they rent from Amazon.

Amazon's insight seems obvious now, but was far less so at the time. As Microsoft's then Chief Software Architect Ray Ozzie said in 2008, "[the cloud services model] really isn't being taken seriously right now by anybody except Amazon." Making the technology, expertise, and economies of scale that went into building Amazon.com available for sale, at rates even an individual could afford was, at the time, a move that baffled the market. No longer would developers need to purchase their own hardware: they could rent it from the cloud.

The decision to make its infrastructure available for pennies on the dollar — literally — did two things. First, it ensured that it would have no immediate competition from major systems vendors. Major enterprise technology vendors are built on margin models; volume sales were of no interest to them. Why sell thousands of servers at ten cents an hour when you can sell a single mainframe for a few hundred thousand? As one senior executive put it, "I'm not interested in being in the hosting business." Much later, these same vendors would later come to see Amazon as a threat.

More importantly, Amazon's cloud efforts gave it an unprecedented ability to recruit developers. Because it was both a volume seller and technology company at its core, Amazon realized the importance of recruiting developers early — moving its entire organization to services-based interfaces. At the time, this was revolutionary; while everyone was talking about "Service Oriented Architectures," almost no one had built one. And certainly no one had built one at Amazon's scale. While this had benefits for Amazon internally, its practical import was that, if Amazon permitted it, anyone from outside Amazon could interact with its infrastructure as if they were part of the company. Need to provision a server, spin up a database, or accept payments? Outside developers could now do this on Amazon's infrastructure as easily as employees. Suddenly, external developers could not only extend

Amazon's own business using their services — they could build their own busi-nesses on hardware they rented from the one-time bookstore, now a newly minted technology vendor.

In pioneering the cloud market, Amazon captured the attention of millions of developers worldwide. Its developer attention is such, in fact, that even vendors that might rightly regard Amazon as a threat are forced to partner with it, for fear of ignoring a vital, emerging market.

This is the power of developers.

GOOGLE

In May 2009 at the conclusion of the second-annual Google I/O conference in San Francisco, then VP of Engineering Vic Gondotra, channeling Steve Jobs, had "one more thing" for attendees: a free phone. In something of a technology conference first, Google gave every attendee a brand new mobile phone, the HTC Hero. Even by industry standards, this was generous; the typical giveaway is a cheaply manu-factured backpack drowning in sponsor logos.

Ostensibly a "thank you" to developers and the Android community, it is per-haps more accurate to characterize this as an audacious, expensive, developer-recruitment exercise. Seventeen months into its existence, Android was an inter-esting project, but an also-ran next to Apple's iPhone OS (it was not renamed iOS until June 2010). Google understood that developers are more likely to build for themselves — what's referred to in the industry as "scratching their own itch" — Google made sure that several thousand developers motivated enough to attend their conference had an Android device to use for themselves.

The statistics axiom that correlation does not prove causation certainly applies here, but it's impossible not to notice the timing of that handset giveaway. On the day that Google sent all of those I/O attendees home happy, the number of Android devices being activated per day was likely in the low tens of thousands (Google hasn't made this data available). By the time the conference rolled around again a year later, the number was around 100,000. By 2011, it was around 400,000. Nine months later, in February of 2012, Google announced at the Mobile World Congress that it was lighting up 850,000 Android devices per day. And just ahead of the release of the iPhone 5, Google disclosed that it was currently activating 1.3 million Android devices daily. It is, by virtually any measure, the fastest-growing operating system in history.

Any number of factors contributed to this success. Google successfully bor-rowed the Microsoft strategy of working with multiple hardware partners to maximize penetration. It made opportunistic hires for its Android team, and it offered high-quality linked services like Gmail, to name just three. But in allocating its capital toward free hardware for developers — a tactic it has repeated multiple times since — Google is telegraphing its belief that developer recruitment was and is crucial to the platform's success. This belief is backed by history: from Microsoft's Windows to Apple's competing iOS, the correlation between operating system and developer adoption has been immensely strong. Few companies, however, have grasped that as deeply as Google, which put its money where its mouth was in courting a developer audience.

MICROSOFT

In a May 2001 address at the Stern School of Business entitled "The Commercial Software Model," Microsoft Senior Vice President Craig Mundie said that the Gnu Public License (GPL) — the license that governs the Linux kernel, among other projects — posed "a threat to the intellectual property of any organization making use of it." A month later, in an interview with the *Chicago Sun-Times*, Microsoft CEO Steve Ballmer characterized Linux as a "cancer that attaches itself in an intellectual property sense to everything it touches." Six years later, Ballmer and Microsoft were on the offensive, alleging in an interview with *Fortune* that the Linux kernel violates 42 Microsoft patents.

In 2009, Microsoft, calling it "the community's preferred license," released 20,000 lines of code under the GPL, intended for inclusion into the Linux kernel. By 2011, Microsoft was testing Linux running on top of its Azure cloud platform. By 2012, Microsoft was in the top 20 contributors to the release of the 3.2 Linux kernel.

While this remarkable about face might seem embarrassing from a public relations perspective, it's simply good business. Microsoft's ability to set its reservations regarding open source aside may in fact be a pivotal moment in the company's history. The epiphany reportedly came in a meeting with Bill Gates in the summer of 2008, a week before Gates retired. His conclusion? Microsoft had no choice but to participate in open source. Credit Gates for understanding that the world had changed around the Redmond software giant. As Tim O'Brien, the General Manager of their Platform Strategy Group told my colleague in February:

We need to think more like the Web.... [O]ne stack to run them all has gone away. This stuff about single vendor stacks is behind us. The days of recruiting developers to where you are is over. You have to go to where they are.

Microsoft remains a firm believer in the virtues of intellectual property and proprietary software. Its strategic understanding of open source was, in a sense, skin deep, in that it did nothing to fundamentally alter the company's DNA. But its understanding that the days of dictating to developers are over is evident in their product strategy.

In the mobile world, Microsoft has implicitly blessed Xamarin, a startup that sells commercially an open source version of their .NET stack. On the cloud, developers can employ Microsoft's .NET stack or erstwhile competitors like Java, JavaScript, or PHP, and build software in the open source Eclipse development environment. And since 2008, Microsoft has been a sponsor of the Apache Software Foundation, an open source governance non-profit.

In other words, the once-dominant Microsoft is adjusting to the shifting landscape; one in which the developers, not the vendors, are in charge. Steve Ballmer, famous for jumping up and down on a stage screaming, "DEVELOPERS! DEVELOPERS! DEVELOPERS!" finally seems to be putting them front and center with the company's strategy.

NETFLIX

In an interview with *Fortune* in 2007, Netflix CEO Reed Hastings summed up his company's future simply, saying "We named the company Netflix for a reason; we didn't name it DVDs-by-mail. The opportunity for Netflix online arrives when we can deliver content to the TV without any intermediary device." In other words, the company's original, popular DVD-by-mail business model that vanquished once mighty Blockbuster was always little more than an intermediary step toward a digital model.

In 1999, Netflix's current path toward online delivery would have been impractical, if not impossible. Not only were content owners years away from accepting the reality that users would find ways to obtain their content online — legally or otherwise — the technology was not ready. As recently as 2005, the year YouTube was founded, the combination of slower home broadband connections and immature video codecs meant that even thirty-second videos were jerky, buffered affairs.

The performance of streaming full-length feature films would have been unacceptable to most customers.

Two years later, however, Netflix was ready. In 2007, Netflix's "Watch Now" — subsequently rebranded "Watch Instantly" — debuted. In a press release, Hastings acknowledged that adoption was a multi-year proposition, but one he felt was inevitable:

> We believed Internet-based movie rental represented the future, first as a means of improving service and selection, and then as a means of movie delivery. While mainstream consumer adoption of online movie watching will take a number of years due to content and technology hurdles, the time is right for Netflix to take the first step.

The age of streaming — and the beginning of the end of DVDs — was here. Four years later, Netflix Watch Instantly would make up almost a third of US Internet traffic. In 2012, the number of movies streamed online is expected to exceed the number of DVD/Blu-Ray discs sold for the first time.

Hastings' original vision was critical because it shaped how the company was built. Netflix wasn't disrupted by a streaming business, because it always saw itself as a streaming business that was biding its time with a DVD rental business. And because a streaming business is, by definition, a technology business, the company has always understood the importance that developers — both those employed by the company, as well as outside developers — could play in the company's future.

Internally, Netflix oriented its business around its developers. As cloud architect Adrian Cockcroft put it:

> The typical environment you have for developers is this image that they can write code that works on a perfect machine that will always work, and operations will figure out how to create this perfect machine for them. That's the traditional dev-ops, developer versus operations contract. But then of course machines aren't perfect and code isn't perfect, so everything breaks and everyone complains to each other.
>
> So we got rid of the operations piece of that and just have the developers, so you can't depend on everybody and you have to assume that all the other developers are writing broken code that isn't properly deployed.

Empowering developers would seem like a straightforward decision, but is hardly the norm. To Netflix's credit, they realized not only the potential of their own technical staff, but what might be harnessed from those not on the Netflix payroll.

Although online retailers enjoy many advantages over brick-and-mortar alternatives, browsing typically isn't one of them. Physical stores are more easily and efficiently navigated than websites limited to the size of a computer screen. As a result, sites like Amazon.com or Netflix rely heavily on algorithms to use the limited real estate of a computer screen to present users with content matched specifically to them. Netflix's own algorithm, Cinematch, attempted to predict what rating a given user would assign to a given film. On October 2, 2006, Netflix announced the Netflix Prize: The first team of non-employees that could best their in-house algorithm by 10% would claim $1,000,000. This prize had two major implications. First, it implied that the benefits of an improved algorithm would exceed one million dollars for Netflix, presumably through customer acquisition and improvements in retention. Second, it implied that crowd-sourcing had the potential to deliver better results than the organization could produce on its own.

In this latter assumption, Netflix was proven correct. On October 8 — just six days after the prize was announced — an independent team bested the Netflix algorithm, albeit by substantially less than ten percent. The 10% threshold was finally reached in 2009. In September of that year, Netflix announced that the team "BellKor's Pragmatic Chaos" — composed of researchers from AT&T Labs, Pragmatic Theory, and Yahoo! — had won the Netflix Prize, taking home a million dollars for their efforts.

A year earlier, meanwhile, Netflix had enabled the recruitment of millions of other developers by providing official APIs. In September 2008, Netflix launched developer.netflix.com, where developers could independently register with Netflix to get access to APIs that would enable them to build applications that would manage users' video queues, check availability, and access account details. Just as Netflix believed that the wider world might be able to build a better algorithm, so too did it believe that out of the millions of developers in the world, one of them might be able to build a better application than Netflix itself.

Why get in the way of those who would improve your business?

5

What To Do? 10 Recommendations

Get To Them Early

Three days after the iPad was released in 2010, a new owner handed his two-and-a-half-year-old toddler the device and videoed the results. That video has been viewed over a million times on YouTube. Besides the statement it makes about the intuitiveness of Apple's design — even toddlers can use the device — the video speaks to the role of technology in our lives today. A generation of children is being raised with iPad and iPhone in hand. Their expectations for user experience may be formed before their fifth birthday. "Baby duck syndrome," according to Wikipedia, "denotes the tendency for computer users to 'imprint' on the first system they learn, then judge other systems by their similarity to that first system." The question vendors should be asking is what happens when "imprinting" occurs before a child can walk?

That problem, fortunately, is relatively specific to consumer technologies. Understandably, very few toddlers are choosing a relational database or web server. But as commercial vendors increasingly compete with open source software alternatives, getting to would-be developers early is vital. When commercial software was all that was available, vendor recruitment of students could be more opportunistic. But as entire crops of students passed through colleges and universities using nothing but open source software, it was no surprise that many went on to build businesses using these same tools instead of their commercial alternatives. As a venture capital partner told a senior executive at a large technology vendor two years ago: "None of the businesses I'm seeing come through are using any of your software. You've got a problem."

The prospect of losing an entire generation of developers for lack of exposure has motivated vendors. Microsoft, for example, courts students with everything from discounted software to college scholarships. In April 2012, in fact, Microsoft ran the "College Puzzle Challenge," a competition in which teams at schools across

North America attempted to be the first to solve puzzles. IBM, for its part, works with universities across the country on research projects, runs student-oriented programs like the IBM Academic Initiative, and offers its software at steep discounts or no cost to students and faculty alike. Google, meanwhile, sponsors the Summer of Code initiative that pairs students with relevant open source projects for brief internships that include mentoring.

At worst, then, you need to be visible during the education process. Your offerings should be price competitive, which in software means free and in hardware means either free or, at worst, on par with cloud offerings. In the best-case scenario, however, your products should be embedded in the students' everyday lives. Apple, for example, is required to expend very little effort marketing itself to students, because it's what they're already using. However you do it, you need to be reaching developers as early in their development as possible.

Algorithmic Recruitment

The simplest way to ensure your success in a developer-dominated world is to ensure that you have high-quality developers. In spite of a number of industries' best efforts, however, recruiting remains systemically inefficient. This is particularly true in the technology space, where well-intentioned but misguided efforts at measuring performance via metrics like lines of code produced can actually do more harm than good.

The good news is that developers are increasingly putting their ability on public display, via open source generally and sites like GitHub specifically. Today, employers often present applicants with awkward coding challenges during interviews to indirectly assess their skill. Tomorrow, they will merely crawl a candidate's public repository, looking at the merits of the code produced. In many cases, in fact, you may be selecting from candidates who indicate their interest in working with you by contributing to your open source project before they're even employees.

Even that manual code-review process might be optimized; in the future, you may not have to look at their code at all. Already, we're seeing signs that that process — the assessment of public code — can be attacked programmatically. Resume.github.com, for example, analyzes a GitHub users' account and provides information about the number of repositories and followers, the breakdown of code by programming language, and more. Matt Biddulph, the developer who sold Dopplr to Nokia, took that to the next level, adding in memory graphs of GitHub user identities and then ranking them algorithmically. The result is short lists of the most influential developers by region. Hiring in Chicago? Algorithmic recruiting can provide short lists of the most desirable developers from a recruiting stand-point, without the overhead and cost of professional recruiters.

When GitHire — a startup inspired by Biddulph's work — promised that it would algorithmically identify five good developers who could be interviewed by phone, it was flooded with more orders than it could fill. As long as developers remain scarce, any more-efficient hiring mechanism will be a substantial competitive advantage.

Open Source and Acqhires

Assume that a startup is acquired strictly for their talent. What should be done with the unwanted or unneeded software assets? In years past, it might have been nominally supported, only to die an ignominious death, forgotten and alone in an unremembered version control system. Today, the preferred approach is to open source the code.

This benefits everyone involved. The company authorizing the release of the asset makes its newly minted employees happy, while receiving goodwill commensurate with the value of the codebase: a fine return on an unvalued asset. The new employees, meanwhile, know that the fruits of their startup labor have the opportunity to live on, and that the organization will allow them to open source software and advance their careers. Having their code public also stands to help their overall visibility and reputation, making them — counterintuitively — more likely to stay. The rest of the world, meanwhile, gets access to code they lacked before.

The open sourcing of code post-acquisition is now standard practice in talent-acquisition scenarios, as discussed previously. After acquiring Powerset, for example, Microsoft gave the employees permission to release the code that is now the top-level Apache project, HBase. Two months after acquiring IndexTank, LinkedIn open sourced its code — as it had promised to do during the transaction. Adobe, meanwhile, contributed PhoneGap to the Apache Software Foundation the day that they announced the acquisition of its parent company, Nitobi.

While it might seem poor business to effectively give away an asset — even an unappreciated one — the logic for acquirers is simple. If the technology assets acquired are non-strategic, the return from releasing the assets as open source code are certain to exceed that of killing them through inattention. The code may or may not find a life beyond its original home within the startup, but the acquirer benefits either way.

Invest in Developer Relations

Born out of government propaganda efforts during the first World War, Public Relations is a profession and a practice that every technology vendor invests in today. As Paul Graham writes:

> One of the most surprising things I discovered during my brief busi-
> ness career was the existence of the PR industry, lurking like a huge,
> quiet submarine beneath the news. Of the stories you read in tradi-
> tional media that aren't about politics, crimes, or disasters, more
> than half probably come from PR firms.

Whether the capabilities are built in-house or outsourced to third-party agencies, and whether the efforts are massive and industry-wide in scope or confined to brochure-ware websites, PR is at worst considered a cost of doing business. Armies of PR staffers are employed to handle and direct inbound informational requests as well as outbound messaging and positioning ranging from email campaigns to press releases to traditional advertising placement. In strategic roles, they're responsible for the entire communication strategy, front to back. These strategies, of course, are intended to cast the vendor or client in the best possible light — hence the alarming over-usage of adjectives like "leading," "innovative," "disruptive," or "dynamic."

By comparison, investments in developer relations — when they're made at all — are typically a small fraction of the wider PR spend. This asymmetrical resource allocation was appropriate for historical software markets. In a market dominated by CIO purchasing, PR is an effective tactic, because executives are more susceptible to traditional marketing and positioning techniques, bread-and-butter tools of PR professionals. PR in such an environment is not just a cost of doing business but, effectively, a form of sales enablement.

As developers have increasingly influenced or outright controlled adoption, however, the efficacy of traditional PR has declined. Developers as a group have proven immune to the majority of traditional software-marketing approaches. Marketing to developers requires a very different approach, and in many cases marketing as it has traditionally been known is simply impossible. Consider the impact of open source. In years past, vendors made bold claims about the performance or functionality of their software, assured in the knowledge that because they controlled access to the product, it would be difficult for would-be customers to independently test these assertions. With open source, however, developers are free to download and test marketing claims on their own, with permission from no one.

PR will remain an important tool in a vendor's arsenal, but in order to target developers, organizations will need to adapt their PR strategies and resource allocation. Ideally, this should be done by complementing them with Developer Relations capabilities.

Embrace Open Source

Ten years ago, businesses were using open source but didn't know it. Five years ago, they were aware that they were using open source, but they didn't realize how much they were using it, and they contributed no source code back. Today, the majority of businesses are not only aware of their open source usage, but approve of it and, increasingly, permit their developers to publish their code as open source software.

That is what they should be doing. Businesses fighting the usage of open source software would have more luck fighting the tide. Where open source offers a credible, competitive solution it should be given every opportunity to succeed, as much for its ability to keep developers happy as for its potential to minimize licensing costs. And where improvements are being made to the code, businesses would be well advised to allow their developers to offer these back to the original project. The alternative is effectively maintaining a fork; each time a new version is released, you'll be obligated to reapply — and test — your external code. The only return from that will be negative.

In cases where the software is an original creation, the evaluation criteria should center on the importance of the software in question. Is it truly differentiating? Is it, like Google's search algorithm, central to how the company makes money? In the majority of cases, the answer to this will be no, and in such cases, releasing the software under an open source license can have multiple benefits.

GitHub's Tom Preston-Werner considers open source code "great advertising," with benefits that include talent identification, attraction, and retention. In a market that's long on demand for talent and short on supply, that by itself should be justification enough. For many businesses, it is. Among developers surveyed by the Eclipse Foundation, for example, more businesses are contributing back to open source than are not (58.2% to 40.1%). The trend toward contribution shows little sign of slowing — between 2007 and 2011, the number of businesses not contributing was down 5.9% while the number of those contributing in some form was up 5.2%.

There are opportunities for embracing open source even for businesses that cannot or do not participate in open source directly. Sponsoring external open source development, as Google does with its Summer of Code program, is another effective tactic. In addition to the hard output — potentially useful software — this offers soft gains in goodwill, talent identification, and recruitment that usually more than offset the costs.

Ultimately, developers are going to use open source whether you like it not. If you want to create a developer friendly atmosphere, then, you must create an open source friendly atmosphere.

Go Global with Your Hiring

Before tools like distributed version control, instant messaging, and Skype existed, working from home was a synonym for taking a day off. Attitudes toward remote workers have shifted over the past decade, even within some of the largest employers in the world. Still, skepticism remains — and with good reason. As Zack Urlocker, COO at Zendesk, puts it: "Distributed development is not cheaper, much harder, but worth it."

At MySQL, there were 400 employees in 40 countries, with 95% of the development staff working from home. The challenges this model presented, from time zone differences to communication technologies to project coordination to legal and commercial logistics, were immense. But it offset these costs with hard savings on real estate, salaries, and improvements in productivity. Most importantly, allowing workers to work remotely is like selling from the Internet: you're no longer limited by your local geography.

As the Gilt Groupe's Chief Administrative Officer Melanie Hughes put it:

> We've actually spread out our technology operations, because in New York it's so hard to get new technologists. The demand is much greater than the supply right now here [in NYC], so we look for places to go with great talent.

With talent markets perpetually short on developers, companies only hiring locally or on a relocation basis are increasingly at a disadvantage relative to competitors that can hire from anywhere in the world. It can be difficult today even to convince developers to commute, let alone relocate to geographies where they're cut off from friends and family. Adaptive organizations, therefore, are seeking ways to leverage distributed development as a core part of their talent-acquisition strategy. If you're not, expect to lose talent to competitors who are.

Lower the Barriers to Entry

Many technologists believe that quality is the most important factor in determining whether a technology is adopted or ignored. And there's no question that the merits of a given product or project are a vital input into the selection process. That has only become more true as open source has made it easier to use and compare code. But quality is just one factor — and it's often not the most important one. Given two technologies, the one that's easier to obtain, configure, and use will usually be the one that wins. Convenience trumps features — even in situations where the more-convenient project is functionally inferior.

By 2005, Sun Microsystems was forced to acknowledge that it had a problem. On one hand, its Java language was dominating within enterprise application development. Sun and hundreds of partners and Java licensees made billions from sales of a combination of hardware, software, and services that helped enterprises create and run the infrastructure they needed to run their businesses. On the other hand, Java was increasingly invisible within web architectures, thanks to a small project originally written by programmer Rasmus Lerdorf to maintain his homepage.

This project, which eventually came to be called PHP, took the Web by storm in the early 2000s, leaving both Java and Microsoft technologies in its wake. By 2003, it was behind more than half the Apache implementations, the most popular web server at the time. Two years later, it was powering over 20 million domains, according to NetCraft's data. It was also the language that popular projects like Drupal and WordPress were written in, and is the language behind massively popular sites like Facebook and Wikipedia.

How did this happen? With millions of Java developers worldwide, why was so little of the Web written in the language? Certainly there were functional reasons: PHP was created for the Web, while Java was not. PHP was an interpreted language, while Java had to be compiled. The syntax of PHP was also easier to learn than Java. But the most important difference of all may have been the fact that PHP was readily available and Java was not.

Due to licensing incompatibilities, Java was practically unavailable to Linux developers. PHP, by contrast — along with Perl and dozens of other programming languages — could be obtained and installed directly from the Linux distribution itself. Developers didn't even have to keep it updated: the operating system's package management system would do that for them.

Faced with a choice between the more mature Java technologies and the convenience of PHP, developers flocked to the latter in droves. Eventually, Sun was compelled to first relicense Java to make it compatible with Linux distributions and then to open source it in an effort to remain competitive. These efforts were successful to a degree — Java remains a popular and widely used technology. But it's worth considering what might have been if Sun's refusal to license Java competitively hadn't opened a door for technologies like PHP to walk through. In all likelihood, they would have found an audience one way or another because they were a good solution. But would it have been an audience 20 million domains strong?

If software adoption is the goal, it's critical to reduce the friction to adoption. Ensure that your software is flexibly licensed, packaged for every potential operating system, available on the cloud, and as usable out of the box as possible. Cloudera, for example, makes its Hadoop distribution available on the cloud and provides packages for virtually every other platform of interest, as well as virtual machine images and raw source code. Whatever a developer's preference, Cloudera's product is easily obtained and installed.

With so many options, it's unlikely that Cloudera will ever lose a developer because of issues around getting the software. If you're making software, make sure that you can say the same thing.

Get into the Game with APIs

When history looks back on Jeff Bezos's career, his greatest business innovation might not be the creation of the world's largest online retailer, the creation of the world's largest cloud business, or the transformation of the publishing industry. It might instead be a decision he laid out in a memo he sent out just after the turn of the century.

According to Steve Yegge, a developer who joined Google from Amazon, Bezos informed his technical staff that henceforth every point of communication within Amazon would be through an interface (API) that could be exposed externally, that there would be no exceptions, and that anyone who didn't follow this rule would be fired. Unsurprisingly, within a few years every service within Amazon was exposed via these APIs. As discussed previously, this not only increased Amazon's own ability to dynamically reassemble its own infrastructure, it meant that Amazon's services could be anyone's services. Individual developers could use Amazon's own servers and storage almost as if they were Amazon employees. Anyone with the time and inclination could build their own storefront, their own application, their own services that drove business back to Amazon. Technologists often talk about the "Not Invented Here" problem: the reluctance to adopt something invented elsewhere. Bezos's mandate was the polar opposite of this: it was a realization that Amazon could never be all things to all people, but that it could enable millions of developers to use Amazon services to go out and target markets that Amazon itself could never reach.

For years, technology vendors relied on business partners to increase their reach; today, businesses turn to developers. Not just technology businesses: all businesses. Everyone from ESPN to Nike to Sears now offers APIs. Why? Because they recognize that they can't do it alone, and perhaps because they're looking at the world around them and seeing that it's increasingly run by software. As Marc Andreessen noted in his *Wall Street Journal* op-ed "Why Software is Eating the World," the world's largest bookseller (Amazon), largest video service by number of subscribers (Netflix), most-dominant music companies (Apple, Spotify, and Pandora), fastest-growing entertainment companies (Rovio, Zynga), fastest-growing telecom company (Skype), largest direct marketing company (Google), and best new movie production company (Pixar) are all fundamentally software companies.

It should be no surprise that even traditional businesses like Sears are trying to become software enabled via APIs. Those that aren't following suit should be. The alternative isn't keeping things the way they are now — it's watching developers help build and extend your competitors' business.

Optimize for Developer Joy

In a presentation at the O'Reilly Strata Conference in 2011, Flip Kromer, CTO and co-founder of data startup Infochimps, discussed the challenges bootstrapped startups face with respect to hiring. Like the Moneyball Oakland A's of Major League Baseball, startups are at a substantial disadvantage in their ability to pay market rates. So, like the Moneyball A's, they need to focus on identifying undervalued assets that they can acquire at a discount and develop into premium talent. One of the most important mechanisms they use in recruitment is optimizing for developer joy.

Some manifestations of this seem fairly trivial; Kromer wrote a custom application called Lunchlady, which aggregates lunch orders for the developers in the Infochimps office (the food is free), including restaurant ratings and order frequency. Others are more serious. Infochimps believes very strongly in code ownership — the idea that developers will work even harder on projects that they personally own, things that they can show to family members and say "I built that." Etsy, the Brooklyn-based craft goods marketplace, has a similar philosophy. Their one hard-and-fast rule for new developers is that they all deploy to production on their first day of employment. They've had to optimize their architecture to adjust for this, but the psychological impact of having a brand-new hire invested in the production system on his or her first day more than justifies the effort.

Developers are also happier when they are working with hardware they like and software they've chosen. Where budgets permit, then, make sure developers get nice hardware that is a pleasure to use. And when it comes to software, the best thing employers can do is to get out of their way. From tooling to infrastructure, developer preferences are strong, and fighting them is not only a losing proposition, it will slow down development. The easier you make a developer's life, the more productive they'll be for you.

And making developers' lives easier doesn't just aid in recruiting efforts — it also makes it harder for developers already on the payroll to leave. GitHub's Zack Holman suggests that employers should "[i]mprison your employees with happiness and nice things and cuddly work processes." GitHub itself does just that with flexible hours, excellent compensation and benefits packages, an enjoyable work environment, an in-house kegorator, and more. The results speak for themselves: incredibly, GitHub has never lost an employee. In a labor market as tight as today's, that's a massive competitive advantage. Hiring is inefficient, onboarding only slightly less so. The less time and fewer resources your company devotes to replacing employees, the larger your advantage over your competitors.

It's possible, of course, to go overboard in pampering your developers. But the correlation between the places that developers want to work and the places that treat their developers well is as obvious as it is undeniable.

Talk with Developers, Not at Them

Engaging with developers is particularly difficult for traditional marketers, because most of their training is lost on that audience. Developers have, out of necessity, built up an immunity to traditional marketing tactics. Print ad placement doesn't work because they spend most of their time online. Online advertising is ineffective because they use AdBlock. Forced registration for white papers fails because they don't care about the white papers. Media messaging is ineffective because the developers know more about the technologies than the reporters do. Analyst webinars are ignored for similar reasons. And if you throw a conference featuring your executives talking about their projects, expect your WiFi to crash as developers tune out the talk and hack their way through the sessions.

Traditional marketing shouldn't be abandoned — it remains a reasonably cost-effective approach for reaching executives, marketers, product managers, and other non-technical audiences. Just don't expect anything other than marginal to negative returns when using these tactics to reach engineering types. As the *Cluetrain Manifesto* suggests, developers don't want to be talked at, they want to be talked with. They don't care about your "message," they care about code.

Businesses that wish to engage developers need to reach out to the developers rather than wait for the developers to approach them of their own accord. Understand where the conversations are happening: in many communities it's Internet Relay Chat (IRC), in others it might be listservs. Broader, less community-centric conversations are happening every minute at developer-centric destinations like Hacker News and Reddit Programming. Part of your developer marketing effort must be listening to channels like these, either directly or through third parties, be they human or algorithm.

From an outbound perspective, marketing materials should consist primarily of either code or documentation. MindTouch, for example, argues that documentation represents potential profit, rather than a cost, because it's not a finely crafted mess of marketing jargon — documentation is legitimately useful from a developer's perspective. As such, it can help you build and sustain communities.

As far as events go, the companies engaging successfully with developers today generally hold non-traditional events. GitHub, for example, is famous for many reasons, not least its "drinkups," which are exactly what they sound like: free drinks for developers and an opportunity to meet and interact with representatives from the company. From 2007–2009, Amazon Web Services ran a series of half-day events called the AWS Start-Up Tour. Apart from the opportunity to hear from the company, it showcased its customers, offering attendees the chance to actively engage and network with other AWS users. And my own company, RedMonk, has staged a pair of successful conferences that combined technology with craft beer — developers do like their beer.

However one intends to market to developers, remember that they cannot be effectively reached using traditional marketing tools. In fact, they can't really be marketed to at all, in the traditional sense of that word. But if they are approached in an appropriately developer-oriented fashion, they will notice.

6

Final Thoughts

Developers and Negotiating with Populations

Developers are the most-important, most-valuable constituency in business today, regardless of industry. Technologists newly empowered with tools, hyper-connected via specialized collaboration and communication networks, and increasingly aware of their own value are no longer content to be mere stage players. They're taking an active hand at direction. That genie is out of the bottle, and will not be returned to it.

Businesses will never have the same control over developer populations that they once did, even if the supply of developers eventually comes closer to matching the demand. Now that developers have finally been handed the tools to control their own destiny, they are taking full advantage and making their influence known, both through the technologies they use and the ones that they ignore. Developers have, in half a decade, propelled Amazon from a mere retailer to a force to be reckoned with. They've pushed formerly dominant businesses like Nokia or Research in Motion to the brink in even less time.

Successful businesses perpetually seek a competitive advantage, an edge over their would-be market rivals. For many businesses, developers will be that edge. Businesses that will be successful over the next decade will be those that understand and appreciate that importance of developers. Whether they're lowering costs and accelerating infrastructure, building the applications that make a platform more compelling, or leveraging the APIs that drive revenues, developers will be the determining factor between success and failure.

However, developers can only represent a competitive edge for a business if they are willing to work with that business. That makes it vital for companies to have smart strategies for engaging with and retaining developers — including both employees and outside developers. Internally, this means acknowledging and approving developers' role in the technology-selection process, rather than combating it. As uncomfortable as that inmates-running-the-asylum narrative might seem, it will be the reality either way. Instead of wasting time and resources fighting the inevitable, empower developers and reap the rewards.

To attract independent developers, businesses must lower their barriers to entry, make their developer incentives clear, and maximize their — and thus their developers' — addressable market. Convenience trumps features, remember, and as Google's Chris DiBona has said, "There is a linear relationship between the number of phones you ship and the number of developers." Market size becomes a self-fulfilling cycle, for better and for worse.

To be on the winning end in the Age of Developers, businesses must understand just how important developers are and then treat them accordingly. When negotiating, remember that developers aren't just another corporate population, they're the New Kingmakers.